careers in a
MEDICAL CENTER

Mary Davis

photographs by
Milton J. Blumenfeld

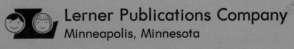

Lerner Publications Company
Minneapolis, Minnesota

LIBRARY OF CONGRESS CATALOGING IN PUBLICATION DATA

Davis, Mary.
Careers in a medical center.

(An Early Career Book)
SUMMARY: Describes the varied careers available in a
medical center, including doctor, registered nurse, medical
secretary, physical therapist, lab technologist, x-ray technician, and administrator.

1. Medicine as a profession—Juvenile literature. 2. Medical
personnel—Juvenile literature. [1. Medicine as a profession]
I. Blumenfeld, Milton J., illus. II. Title.

R690.D38   610.69   72-7651
ISBN 0-8225-0310-7

International Standard Book Number: 0-8225-0310-7   Library of Congress Catalog Card Number: 72-7651

Fourth Printing 1976

48507

Would you like to work in a medical center?

Medical centers are busy places. Every day, hundreds of people come to medical centers for health care. Some people come for check-ups. Others come to have their eyes examined. And some people come to medical centers to have operations. Medical centers also help people who have had accidents and need treatment right away.

Many people with special skills work at medical centers. There are doctors, nurses, X-ray and laboratory technicians, and pharmacists. Each person's job is very important.

In this book, you will learn about some of the jobs in a medical center. If you are the kind of person who would like to make people feel healthy and happy, you might like to work in a medical center.

MEDICAL RECEPTIONIST

The first person you see when you go to a medical center is the medical receptionist. He or she greets patients, keeps records, and makes appointments. Because a medical receptionist talks to so many people every day, he or she must be friendly and understanding.

Most medical receptionists have had some office training.

MEDICAL SECRETARY

Medical secretaries are very important people in a medical center. They gather information about the patients and put the information into files. Medical secretaries also type letters for the doctors and do other important office work.

Medical secretaries usually have special secretarial training. They must also be able to understand medical words.

REGISTERED NURSE (RN)

Registered nurses are highly skilled people who know a lot about medicine. They are trained to work closely with doctors in giving medical care. Registered nurses give shots and pills, and carry out important tests that tell about the health of a patient. Registered nurses give patients very special attention and put them at ease.

Registered nurses take special courses in nurses' training. If you like to help people, you would make a good registered nurse.

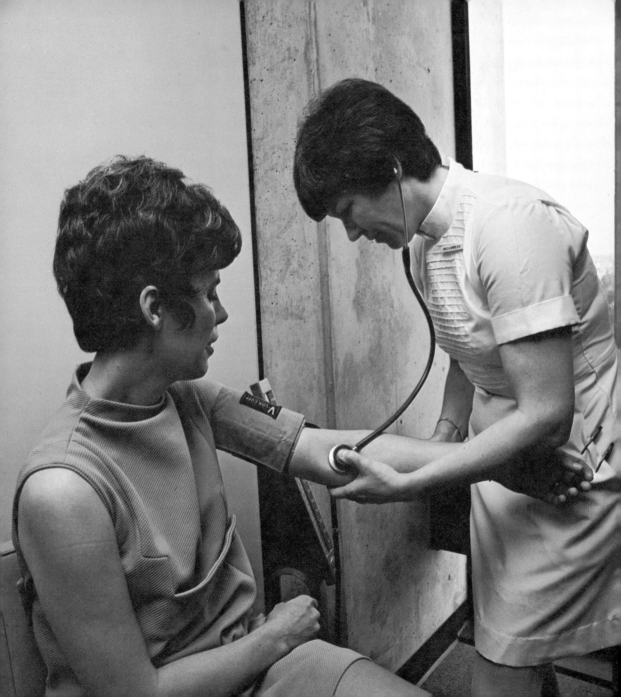

LICENSED PRACTICAL NURSE (LPN)

Licensed practical nurses are a lot like registered nurses. They prepare people for examinations, take their temperatures, and try to make them feel comfortable. They also assist the registered nurses and doctors.

Like registered nurses, licensed practical nurses take special nurses' training but go to school for shorter periods of time. Licensed practical nurses work in nursing homes and hospitals as well as in medical centers. They work wherever medical care is provided.

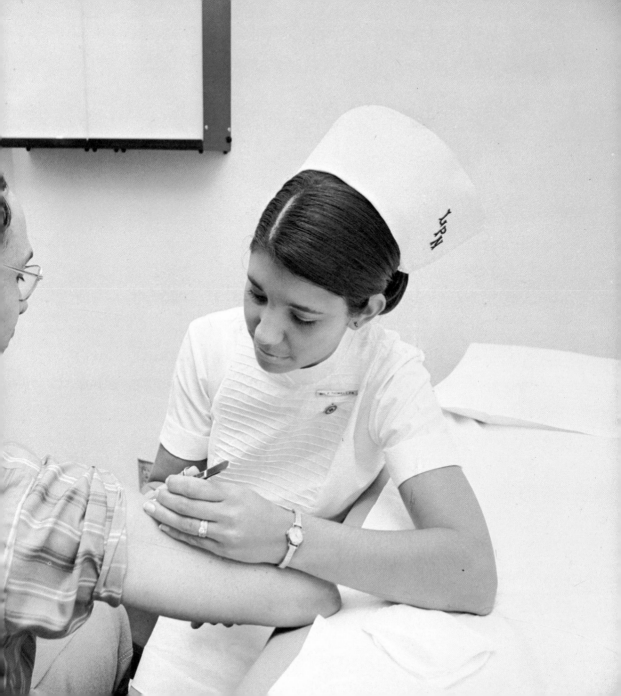

DOCTOR

There would be no medical centers if there were no doctors. When you are sick, doctors try to make you well. There are many kinds of doctors in a medical center. One kind of doctor takes care of your eyes, another takes care of your skin. Still others take care of bones and muscles and internal organs. All of the doctors work together to keep you healthy.

Doctors spend many years in medical training. They work many hours a day to give people the best care possible.

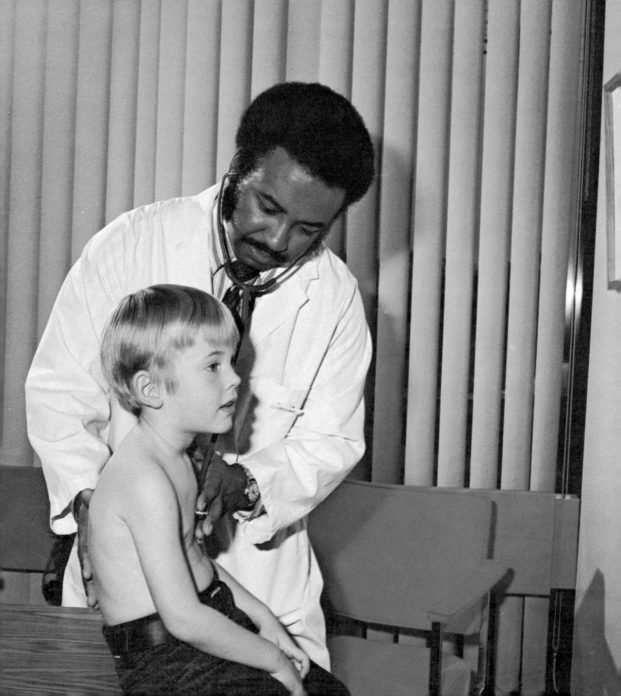

DOCTOR'S ASSISTANT

A doctor's assistant helps the doctor. One of the assistant's jobs is to examine the people who come to the medical center for check-ups. This saves time for the doctor who must help people with special problems.

Doctors' assistants sometimes have special training, or they may get their training as they work in the medical center.

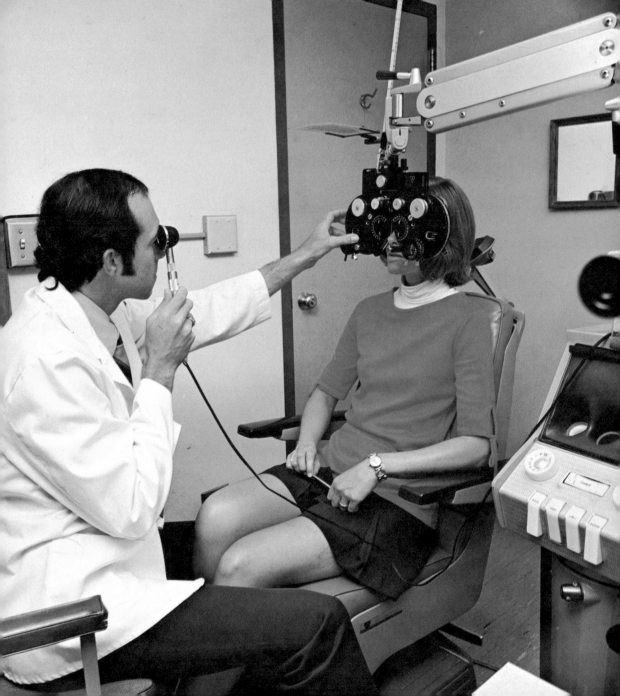

SURGEON'S ASSISTANT

The surgeon's assistant helps the *surgeon*, the doctor who operates on patients. The surgeon's assistant prepares the patient for the operation and helps the surgeon during the operation. He or she may also help the surgeon put casts on broken arms and legs. The surgeon's assistant in the picture is helping the doctor put a cast on a patient's broken foot.

Many surgeon's assistants receive their medical training in the military service.

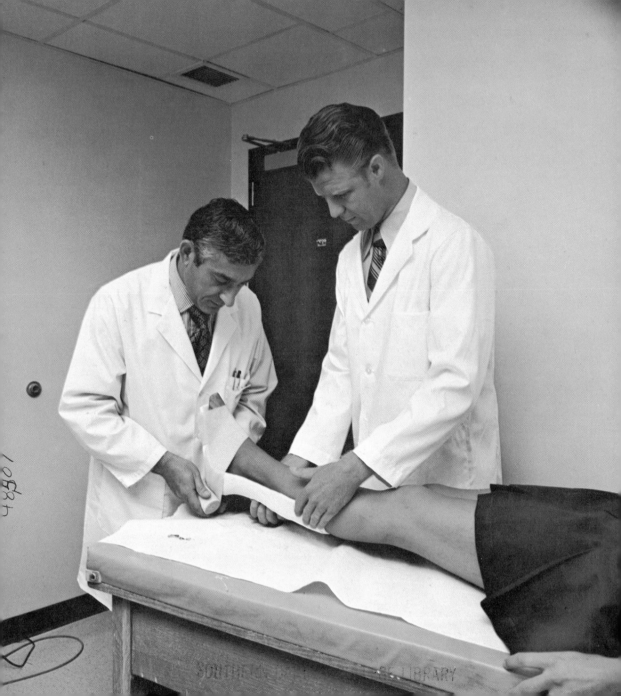

PHYSICAL THERAPIST

Physical therapists treat patients with injuries or diseases that restrict movement. They know many ways to get damaged muscles in the body to work right again. One of these ways is to rub the spot that hurts. The physical therapist in the picture is rubbing the muscles in the patient's shoulders and neck.

Physical therapists have college degrees. Almost all of their college courses relate to the work they will do when they graduate.

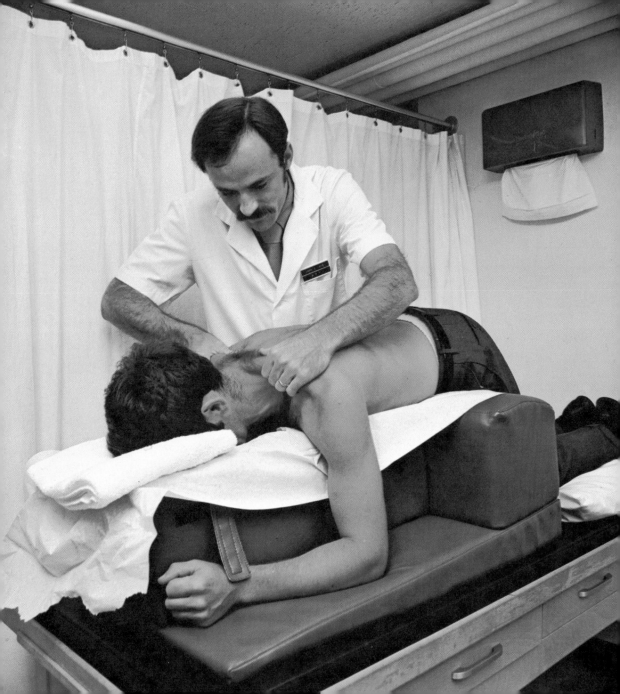

LAB ASSISTANTS

If you like science, you might like to be a laboratory assistant. Lab assistants give tests to patients that tell the doctors about the patients' health. One of these tests is a blood test. In a blood test, the lab assistant takes a sample of blood from the patient's finger or arm.

Sometimes young people are afraid to have blood tests. Lab assistants help them to understand that there is nothing to be afraid of.

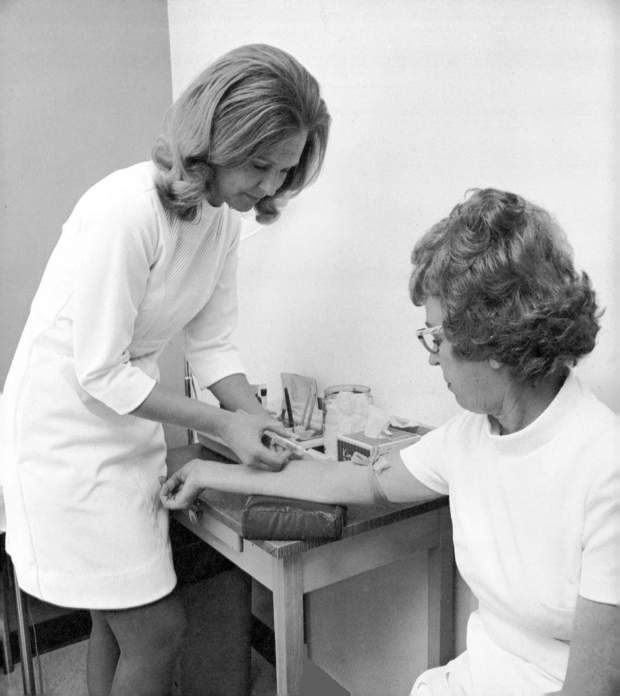

LAB TECHNOLOGIST

Lab technologists are really scientists. They know all about the germs that make people ill. Lab technologists study blood samples that the lab assistants take during blood tests. By studying a patient's blood, lab technologists can tell what kind of illness a patient has.

Lab technologists must know how to operate special equipment in the laboratory.

PHARMACIST AND PHARMACIST'S ASSISTANT

When you are ill and your doctor wants you to take medicine, he or she will give you a *prescription*. This is a note that describes what kind of medicine you need. Pharmacists are people who prepare your medicine. They know all about drugs and medicine. Pharmacists must have special licenses before they can work. They must be able to prove that they can do a good job.

Pharmacists' assistants wait on patients and put labels on their medicine bottles. Each label tells what kind of medicine is in the bottle, how much should be taken, and when it should be taken.

X-RAY TECHNICIAN

X-ray technicians use special equipment to take pictures of the inside of a person's body. Like photographers, X-ray technicians must place patients in the correct position in order to get good pictures. The pictures sometimes help the doctors decide what is wrong with their patients.

X-ray technicians are highly skilled. They must know all about X-ray equipment.

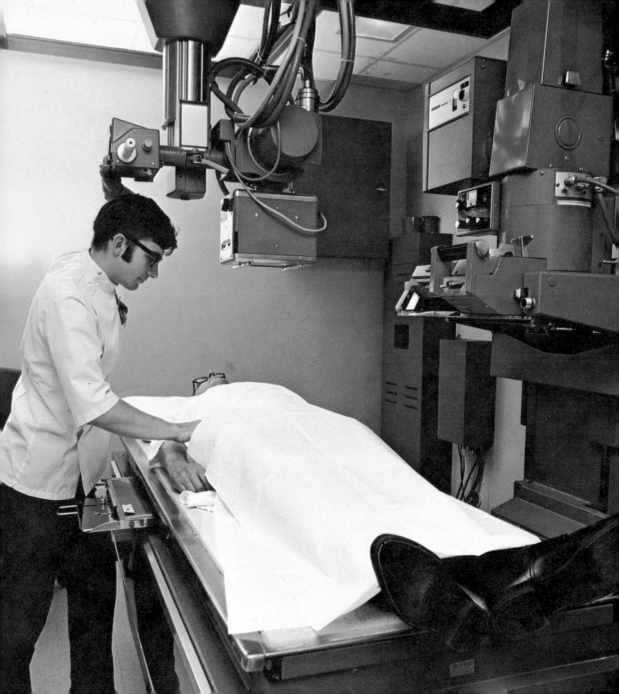

MEDICAL RECORDS CLERK

Medical records clerks seldom see patients. But they see all the patients' files. The files contain information about each patient's health. Medical records clerks keep the files up to date. When a doctor asks for a certain patient's file, a clerk gets it from the file room.

Medical records clerks who work in big medical centers handle hundreds of files every day! High school graduates are often trained for this job.

BUSINESS OFFICE CLERK

People who have been treated at a medical center pay their bills at the business office. The business office clerk accepts their money and gives them *receipts*— notes that show the bills have been paid. The clerk also helps them fill out important papers.

The business office clerk usually has secretarial or business training. He or she likes to work with people.

INSURANCE, CREDIT
COLLECTIONS

PATIENT INSURANCE
CLAIM FORMS

MEDICAL CENTER ADMINISTRATOR

The men and women who are administrators make sure that the medical center is doing the best job it can do. For example, medical administrators see to it that the medical center has good equipment and supplies. They decide how the medical center should use its money. They decide when to hire more doctors and nurses. They also make sure that the building is in good condition. And if more space is needed, they think of ways to provide it.

The medical center administrators know how important a good medical center is to the people of their city.

Medical center careers described in this book

Medical Receptionist

Medical Secretary

Registered Nurse (RN)

Licensed Practical Nurse (LPN)

Doctor

Doctor's Assistant

Surgeon's Assistant

Physical Therapist

Lab Assistant

Lab Technologist

Pharmacist and Pharmacist's Assistant

X-ray Technician

Medical Records Clerk

Business Office Clerk

Medical Center Administrator